Fall Sanctuary

© 2005 by Jeff Hardin
First Printing

Published by Story Line Press
PO Box 1240, Ashland, Oregon 97520-0055
www.storylinepress.com

This publication was made possible in part thanks to the generous
support of our individual contributors.

Cover art: Winslow Homer (American, 1836–1910)
Gathering Autumn Leaves, c. 1878, Oil on canvas
97.2 x 61.6 cm (38 1/4 x 24 1/4 in.)
Cooper-Hewitt, National Design Museum,
Smithsonian Institution
Gift of Mrs. Charles Savage Homer, Jr., 1917-14-3
Photo: Mildred E. Baldwin

Book design by Sharon McCann

Library of Congress Cataloging-in-Publication Data
Hardin, Jeff, 1968–
Fall sanctuary : poems / by Jeff Hardin.
p. cm.
ISBN 1-58654-043-2 (alk. paper)
I. Title.

PS3558.A623F35 2004
811'.54--dc22
2004019385

Fall Sanctuary

Jeff Hardin

Story Line Press
Ashland, Oregon

Grateful acknowledgment is offered to the following journals where some of these poems appeared, sometimes in slightly different versions:

Ascent: "To a Crawdad"; *The Bloomsbury Review:* "Genealogy"; *Iron Horse Literary Review:* "Elder Poet's Final Tour"; *Mid-American Review:* "The Babe"; *New Millennium Writings:* "An Old Quarrel Put to Rest"; *New Orleans Review:* "After So Long Taking the Same Road," "Love Poem for My Being Here at All"; *The New Republic:* "Summons"; *Nimrod:* "Enamored"; *Ploughshares:* "Passover"; *PoetryNet:* "No Need for Alarm"; *Puerto del Sol:* "Reply to the Shhh in the November Grass"; *Rattapallax:* "Morning and Night"; *Smartish Pace:* "Lady of Wealth, Circa 1963"; *Sou'wester:* "Love Poem for Moonlit Backyard"; *West Branch:* "Among the Giants of East Main Pool Hall"; *Zone 3:* "Pasture."

"After So Long Taking the Same Road," "An Old Quarrel Put to Rest," "Breathing Exercise," "Enamored," "Genealogy," "Summons," and "To a Crawdad" previously appeared in *Deep in the Shallows*, a chapbook published by GreenTower Press, 2002.

For their friendships and generous spirits across the years, I gleefully thank the following people: Wilmer Mills, Timothy Geiger, Ruth Ellen Kocher, Bill Brown, G'anne Harmon, Alice Sanford, Lola White, Elizabeth Hahn, Victoria Clausi, Anne Doolittle, Josh Russell, Katherine Smith, and Lisa Coffman. A special thanks to David Till, who first took me into the house of being. And gratitude to Mark Jarman, for noticing.

For Starla, Storie and Eli

&

with praise for the life of
Marie Melson
1910–2004
(second pew, first seat)

CONTENTS

❧ INTRODUCTION ❧
by Mark Jarman

Mostly Gratitude

Theodicy argues that despite the existence of evil, God remains not only good but omnipotent. For Jeff Hardin, God and creation are one, they are the world, and evil would keep us from accepting it and one another. His poem "Theodicy" argues his position as follows:

See, this magnolia bloom,
its petals thick and rubbery,
tenacious, not easily cast aside,
so much fragrance
I get a little giddy
just breathing in its presence—
this is the manner of world
we wake to every day. . .

Hardin's world is primarily the rural South, and his people primarily country people with their deep and rooted knowledge, like his grandmother who can say of dogwoods, "The hotter the sun the whiter the bloom." Out of his world and its speech he makes lyric poetry of praise for the earth:

spring revying up
            like nobody's business,
bloom after bloom after bloom after bloom,
no room for dark or blemish
                    even in the darkest hearts.

"Something in my brain is washed by sunlight," he tells us in "Genealogy," and in "Late Spring Sanctuary," "mostly gratitude's my theme." Yes, mostly. Even though he says, "I am no

9

romantic," Hardin is one, but with a modern difference. "I fell asleep in childhood and awoke to meetings I must attend," he writes in "This Earth We Walk Upon." That difference is a stoic refusal to whine or yearn. The object in his poetry is to understand: "I know what I know," he admits at the end of one poem, "and I want to know more."

A young poet wears his influences on his sleeve. The Wrights are there on Hardin's—both James and Charles, the compassion of the former, the music of the latter, plus a drollery that is Hardin's alone. He can make a crawdad a fit subject for a sonnet ("everybody's childhood boasts / an afternoon of chasing you"), and in one of his most remarkable poems, "The Babe," he turns the great ball player into a philosopher.

It's flooding somewhere tonight in America,
the Babe is thinking. *Another crop*
down the drain. He looks up and the ball
hangs there, supple, a sphere, Earth itself
as if seen from orbit, its oceans and land
distinct. *Faith's an enigma,* the Babe thinks.
Loneliness makes everything into a mirror.

And in "To a Crawdad," he concludes, "Older, we now emulate / your style: something chases us and we retreat."

In the end it is simply a pleasure to listen to Hardin think in his poems, even as he deprecates himself ruefully as a "small-time metaphysician of the wee hours." The stoic realist is always reminding the romantic of the fundamental nature of things:

We tell ourselves it's not the destination
but the journey,
        the being-where-one-is.
That's a stretch. That's a get-down-on-one's-knees-
and-feel-around.
        That's the poetry in us talking.

I welcome the poetry that talks in Jeff Hardin, who can look at desolation and remark, "Even a bottle cast out along the roadside will see itself / eventually filled." A believer's lyrics, his are the songs of one who has accepted the world for what it is, mostly—a gift.

And it came to pass, that, while they communed
together and reasoned, Jesus himself drew near, and
went with them. But their eyes were holden that they
should not know him. And he said unto them:
What manner of communications are these that ye have
one to another, as ye walk, and are sad?
—Luke 24: 15-17

IN FEAR AND TREMBLING

after Milosz

Not that I, within myself,
possess the power to bestow permission,
but if I could I would. *Live long,*
I'd say. *Believe in joy, the fullness of it.*
Perceive each hour as a threshold.
I'm not naïve enough to think that this
would be the end of our remorse.
There'd still be women on the streets
pulling shawls about them in the freezing cold.
Hitler would have set aside his paint brush anyway.
We cannot halt a record week of touch-downs
on the plains, houses obliterated,
unread letters strewn a hundred miles away.
But the fact a voice can speak a language
and be understood by someone else
is itself incomprehensible, and surely evidence
of compassion that exists outside ourselves.
Or do we just prefer this fallen world,
where we strive against the other's interests
and guard ourselves and know that we're alone?

EARLY SPRING SANCTUARY

Inexplicably,
the yellow pansies are angelic,
realizations ground-bursting here and there,
spring revving up
                    like nobody's business,
bloom after bloom after bloom after bloom,
no room for dark or blemish
                                        even in the darkest hearts.

Mine, for instance,
all falter and lost gleam, pious-purged,
drenched in the ooze
                    of the commonplace.
None of that today, though.
None tomorrow.
Day after next...who knows?

February filled the water table.
March was mild and waiting for its due.
April, too,
        afternoon palettes adding hues and bold lines.

Can't help but think of Moses,
Heston-bearded and singed by God's shadow—
one strike on the rock,
the water set to issue forth,
one strike,
        the Promised Land kept past his reach.

And you and I—nameless sun-lovers, responsible for no one,
going the ways we wish to go—
wake these mornings to pink azaleas,
grass so thick
                we'd never count the blades,
each full and green, disputing nothingness.

Hardly seems fair, hardly seems righteous,
but I stretch out on the lawn's candescence
and stare up through
                the lush of what's around me,
green buds on the dogwoods,
spillage of honeysuckle,
                iris-tipsy and begonia-blessed
and I'll take it, I'll take it, I'll take it.

✿ SUMMONS

Word comes today along the lengths of rain
and through the shiver-spray of hedge-rows.
All my life I've listened, not always for a human voice.
Sometimes I've heard the cool sleep of ferns.

A little seems left out of whatever is or isn't.
Even in my woods I am at best a stir.
Whatever the leaves wish to do with me
I won't be found akilter, nor plaintive.

For trees their shape must be reward—jut, hoist,
spurn and leap, gape, harden. For trees,
their highest parts mingle. Some thoughts
must be tracked like a snow-field near dusk.

There are too many empty boats in Japanese paintings.
What does this hold, given the eighteen months
my child has been a presence on the globe?
With precision, the right tone, can a question be an altar?

I feel spoken to some days and unable to respond.
Mist ennobles all participants no matter the scene.
Yellow, the most medicinal of colors, seems to weep
on behalf of many in the world not near themselves.

PASSOVER

The hotter the sun the whiter the bloom,
     my grandmother used to say of the dogwoods,
     Christ's trees, still bearing his blood,
and our hearts, of course,
               in need of redemption.

On her cue, I'd wield a bowl of potato peels
     out past the barn to the hog pen
     where sows snout-rooted mud-slime
and anything I threw them,
               squealing indescribable glee.

I've spent my lifetime thinking on sin,
     on the dark place a heart is
     and the mind trying its best to slant it
otherwise, two prongs
               like a snake's strike.

I've spent my lifetime shuffled back and forth—
     in awe of the leaf-shape, the fungus-browned bark;
     seeing everything as moral, as indictment of self.
Which is it?
           the thing as itself? or the lesson it teaches?

I'm thirty-three now, the age of Jesus when he said,
     "It is finished." At night the crickets deem the universe
     a simple place of ease, a drift toward the next day's
brilliance of light.
           I wake and undo. I pray these little blasphemes.

LOVE POEM FOR THE ABSOLUTE

At times I entertain myself,
thinking of a mid-morning walk,
the kind that navigates
                    idleness and oak limbs,
what's left of remembering and the incomplete days.

One step, and I disintegrate—one step and I blaze.
One step—
          I enter light like a sapling dreams.

First things first—or is it last things last?
Either way,
          the boy I was is dead.
I heard him groan his last when the solitude stalled.
He called to a trust, then sank when none replied.

At times I am no more,
                    just a wisp in the air,
a slipped-free note, a willow leaf turned to dust
on the ground rot. Keep it moving,
o tour guide, keep it moving.

The minutes let their eyelids droop, and I live.
The minutes bed down,
                    and the room I am goes dark, dark.

GENEALOGY

No one back at the house, I wander out, cross the fence,
follow the paths the cows have made their own.
Something in my brain is washed by sunlight,
a yellowing-inward of warmth and searching;
and I stand on a knoll where a shack used to be,
a century ago, when a man and a woman lying down at night
could hear, despite the crickets, the stillness of the other.
I think, inside me, a tenderness exists,
bound to vines the fencerow makes a home for
and to the trace of air in the hickory nut's hull.
I belong to barns, which belong to weather and weeds
and the careful years that do their best but lose us.

AFTER SO LONG TAKING THE SAME ROAD

this morning he has turned, not far from home,
onto a road which sneaks along a ridge a while,
then presents a bridge, one-laned and ancient,
over a dingy river and on through fields. This early,
a fog erases much he'd wish to see, but every few yards
a break appears and offers plowed dirt or bluff,
and he feels redeemed to be on earth—a sentiment he would
surely deny if word got back—for it's been years
since a smell so thick of honeysuckle came over him.
Like the holy ghost, he thinks, nectar-throated.
Such a scene, he knows, is *presence* in a way we aren't,
and remarkable now are zones a spirit passes through.
Each word, in its own way, is a form of Amen.
Later, though, when he faces what the workday wants of him,
time feels not at all enlarged: neither stray nor lucid,
neither stirred nor unruly nor beseeching nor apt.

LATE SPRING SANCTUARY

Quiet porch, cool wind through the slats,
but in a month
                    the heat will shrink the leaves,
and what I'll sign my name to then
won't be this hour's hillside.

So far, about this life, I can't complain.
Oh I can a little,
                    stiff-lipped against impermanence
and riled the stars can't answer back,
but mostly gratitude's my theme.

I'm out of step, I know, and sentimental,
and while I'm at it
                    why not also grandiose,
and touched, and rosy-eyed,
and duped to think it's all divine?

The café bombs, I understand, still detonate,
and babies enter stillborn—
                    no touch can bring them back.
The flames lick just enough the loved one doesn't die,
and one who plummets crushes someone late for home.

Some days what's beyond my grasp
                            seems to be a guide.
I live not unmended, mercy-flushed and sometimes mournful,
steeped in radiance, sometimes eloquent,
the self and Abyss in their sweet back and forth.

PASTURE

It's easy to be humble here
where the filled udders of cows
swag beneath their lumbering bulks.

I am reminded of a man
—Thoreau I think we called him—
who could stand (it is said) for hours,
listening to the reedy sounds
and reminders of why he came
—not to the pond or to the field,
but to the womb and into the world.

If we think of the soul,
we think of it in jeopardy.

I think I'll walk on down this way
and see behind what foliage
heaven kept itself last night.

FROM HERE TO THERE

My father wrestles with the chain, slams it
tangled toward the truckbed where it catches
tailgate, slither-clangs to a heap beneath
his feet. Like a serpent of heavy links.
Like the unwieldy weight his bogus life
has been, his trying to move it from here
to there. He curses God, who made him fail.
He turns, commands me pick up what I can.

I do: his stubborn will, his quiet code,
the all day bouts of walking through the yard
to find out what the moles have thieved. The stare.
The muscle pulled. The knife slammed down to hush
the dinner talk. I've heaved to get to here,
mid-life, his life, to pack it up for good.

TO ANYONE WHO'LL LISTEN

for Roger

Old Doc said, "Come on in," his home a bus
on blocks above a filthy creek. His flour
and meal in Folgers cans, which kept them dry,
he bragged. His bed: a couch. Cracked panes. Wood stove.

To anyone who listened he sang Hank.
He held his pick like a coin he'd lost, then found.
"To die in a Cadillac," he said, "would be
just fine," then asked if I could buy him booze.

I know: I have betrayed him telling this.
Perhaps his story's used to bolster mine.
Old Doc, you're right: my heart has told on me.
I've turned our past into a myth for show.

You took me in your arms, breathed whiskey, wept,
said, "Don't forget me." But I had to. And can't.

FOOL'S GOLD

In the slush-heat of summer,
                    the wind-loss and stall,
I gathered and piled the fool's gold,
a boy on a mission
                    at the pasture's edge.

It didn't matter that I couldn't purchase a thing.
It didn't matter
                    mother wakened in the doorway
in robe and slippers, calling me in
to bologna and liverwurst—

I had the flecks on my hands,
                    on my shirt
and my shoes. No telling toward where
I might have squandered my fortune.

On the road the log trucks
                    bumped and geared-down,
their red flags cursive in wind—illegible, illusive,
the deep south moving
                    toward another scarce paycheck.

Under the eaves,
                    the wasps tease-tapped the hour,
though a broom-swish and slap
sent them yard-dizzy,
                    one or two crushed clean out of themselves.

Now when I think of it,
                    I was saying farewell:
dig and hoist free—dust and wash clean;
store up what no one
                    would think worth the fuss.

When I think of it, the stump-skirts blaze beyond sight—
and a young boy starts walking
                    the rim of the far-off.

FOLLOWING AFTER

Along the back roads, I test the curves thrown wide
then stitched back in,
                              rising toward the hills,
toward the ghost shapes of pine,
orderly, existential.

Paper mill country.
                              Twenty years then pulp.
Trucks going in and trucks coming out.

This dusk finds me desultory, shucked-off.
The road's unreachable even when we're on it.
It goes toward its focus
                              and hauls us behind.

Its form is composed of the jumbled and scattered,
what somehow still
                              gets us near the sublime.
Barn. Ditch. Ford Fairlane on blocks.
Middle Bridge looming,
                              scaffolding.the flow.
Something through the brush, out of range, out of range.

I've chased the years the way my father did,
slow crawl past Joe Love's store,
gear jerk
           over the bridge to Piney,
the roads arterial, coated with county dust.

Same old narrative as his,
                              a little moonlight thrown in,
river smell breeze-lodged and constant.

The old man knew his stuff, they say,
could steer through the channel from memory alone,
take the head of the barge
                          and nudge it, ease it,
all the way in without touching the lock wall,
in the deep deep dull of 3 a.m.,
Whitley in the background,
                          no stranger to the rain.

I'm following after in my own quiet way,
doing my part
                          in the family's loose lineage.
Nudge a word here. Steer toward the deep.
Thirty years behind
                          and a little too Lethean.

But we don't get the road map ever in time.
Only later. Only after—after and always only after.
We get the monotone
                          of life's swift answer,
gut-stabbed, wedged where we can't grab a hold.

I've spent the years tracing back
to my father's slow ways,
born from the river,
                          its driftwood, its distance,
from his watching, for a living, the *ease-past* and *dazzle*.

Dusk has it own course, a daily deduction.
These wheels give it hell
                          and a merciful hush.
I've fought with the devil, got down on his level.
But through it all, I go where I'm going.
I know what I know,
                          and I want to know more.

THIS EARTH WE WALK UPON

There are those who (God help us) rob the graves of flowers.
What hymn is sung then when their hands are reaching down,
and is that you and I standing to the side, urging them on?

We were never told, but the amaryllis is recompense
for this earth we walk upon. We were never told
the soul moves counter-clockwise—it rewrites plot.

I fell asleep in childhood and awoke to meetings I must attend.
All day, it seems, I wait for the clean, crisp sound
of apples bitten into, that lust-intake of trellis-juices.

I've been slow to be the being I'm becoming.
I'm mostly pause and flash and anonymity;
leaflet and plunge; rein being held at the open gate.

And as ever, despite no longer crawling through ditch grass
as when a child, I'm in awe of brief time and its generosities,
to which I reach and can't-help-myself plunder.

✿ ONLOOKER

He thought for sure
every thought
would come again,
just with
a different tone.

So what did it matter
if Dostoevsky
dwelled on guilt?

Or if Tu Fu
missed his home,
drank his wine,
heard rain slipping
through the folds
of the wind?

The world spinning
made it possible
to walk a path
without vertigo.

This same world contained
corners and pockets,
tucked-away places
—in each one
someone looking outward,
imagining.

Perhaps all we do
is walk back and forth
between the window
and our need
to be outside.

THEODICY

See, this magnolia bloom,
its petals thick and rubbery,
tenacious, not easily cast aside,
so much fragrance
I get a little giddy
just breathing in its presence—
this is the manner of world
we wake to every day:
small revelations, curling and intricate;
and what should we become then,
how speak to one another,
how move beyond these faces
we prepare, if such a world exists?

LOVE POEM FOR MOONLIT BACKYARD

I am no romantic,
                    unless you ask my friends,
but what do they know, wise-acres and grumps,
jaded past all comprehension.
So I stand here—big deal—
high on the back deck,
                    lit in the moonlight,
small-time metaphysician of the wee hours.

A friend says not to love this world
too much,
                    to find no counsel
in the river's rise, the hummingbird's poise
at the lip of the bloom,
                    no joy in the snail trail,
the porpoise nudge, the deer rub, the ice thaw.

Call my standing here, if you must, a rebuttal
against the dead places
                    kept inside me,
against the clock whose motion
my cells
          are in cahoots with.

I resign my allegiance to most anything
well-received
                    and hope to be shuffled off
under cover of cedars and oaks
to that place where nothing is dim
or not known
                    or ever again lacking the imprint
the moonlight tried to convey as fact.

So much quiet evening ought to get us
somewhere,
              nothing but breeze-shimmerings
and sun-lapse, trees in the same spot
decade after decade. Dirt dauber
sketches up the porch rail, little da Vinci
of the bump-against, the nestle-toward.

So snug am I in the endlessness of life.
So trampled are the faint of heart in this world,
though one long look at the sky
                            could do us all in.
When we sleep tonight, parasites on the back of the void,
will dreams be surged with wisdom?
Will morning light find us supplicant,
our inventories
              spread out uncertainly?

TO A CRAWDAD

No one much will love you, except perhaps
to eat, and this is sad. You live in mud
and slime, and no one knows your morning mood,
if you have one. The creek bed, with its heaps
of rocks, obscures your life from ours, although
(most likely) everybody's childhood boasts
an afternoon of chasing you: the quick-tests
and splashes left and right, wondering how
so swiftly your elusiveness could clear
in sudden dust. Older, we now emulate
your style: something chases us and we retreat.
Our stirrings settle back. We create more.
All the while we move backwards into life,
timidly, though the shadow feared is a leaf.

❧ ENAMORED

For many years now, maybe more,
I've wished to be forthright about the elm.
I've mistook its leaves for prayers,
which in this world is rather easy.
Its trunk shall never depart this life,
even if lightning proves the sky,
or drought makes many weep,
or pestilence widens its shadowy throat.

And I am a fan of gravity's care,
that we are mostly held in place,
that though we rush and conjure days
we have no cause to think are ours,
still something unseen is faithfully near.
Even the buzzard's descent I love,
the back-flap of wings to stall its fall,
the feet-clutch and rise, the remainder.

Could we call this a life, if minus the pond
catching its ripples of rain? May I stay
forever here, may catbrier and mud
be my nuptials for now, may the night
unleash its odor of moon and nearby field;
for I've distinguished the whisk of bat wings
all around me, circumscribing, and I am
enamored to be included, attended, steered past.

A great admirer am I of stump and fence post,
of cowbell, hollow log, magnolia bloom
and creek bed shale. I am not cast down
when tombstones rear. No matter the dates
I'm pleased, if not ecstatic. I claim solace

because a fiddle knows its range and not my own,
because beyond is so much called innumerable
I can't begin to begin, though I would and I have...

THE BABE

Babe Ruth steps to the plate,
winks at the pitcher like he's looking
in a mirror, like this of all days
has light enough for all involved.
The Babe raises his long bat
toward the cheering fans beyond the fence,
just to remind himself, to keep steady
that place inside so frequently
senseless and elsewhere.
The Babe would rather be on a bus,
be one of the faces briefly seen,
murmuring only to itself, remembering
clothes hung on a make-shift line,
the one sock mateless out on the end.
It's flooding somewhere tonight in America,
the Babe is thinking. *Another crop
down the drain.* He looks up and the ball
hangs there, supple, a sphere, Earth itself
as if seen from orbit, its oceans and land
distinct. *Faith's an enigma*, the Babe thinks.
Loneliness makes everything into a mirror.
He can see the pitcher's leg sidle-sling, plop
and stir the dust. The Babe steps forward.
The Babe swings. In a gallery, not far from here,
a woman composed of paint and otherwise real
looks nonchalantly downward. A diamond
punctuates her turned neck—turned
for what reason, toward or away from whom?
A window must be near. Or another season.
Children on a sidewalk can be heard
drawing lines for hopscotch. Rain is days away.
The crowd rises to its aching, adamant feet.

Someone has remembered why he's here,
and it's infectious and involves screaming.
The Babe feels his own chin turn, a force,
an exultation toward the faint thing
the heart makes a temple for.
Men have died crawling through barbed wire,
having hours before written letters home.
Windmills, without wind, stand motionless
on the plains. No two moments ever knew
one another, though side by side.
The Babe thinks, *In the soul
is everything soluble?* He steps
into the baseline and the grooves
in the infinite miles of memory suddenly present.
The Babe sometimes feels like a sheep
on a hillside, way up, like a dreamed thing.
Pure going now, rounding first base,
he's like a landscape unto himself,
moving silent and unmistaken across the globe.
He remembers the sound behind the sound of cheering.
He hears the dust falling through his name.

❋ LOVE POEM FOR THE BEGINNING AND END OF IT ALL

I don't care what September says;
I sit outside,
        let the sweat say its peace
down the bare-wind coolness
at the back of my neck.

All day no one has a clue for what to say,
not even a hum
        toward the shape it could be,
none, none at all,
though heaven sits and waits for us to eavesdrop,
though all words begin
        with a single phoneme.

Maple leaves all browning and brittle,
a shapelessness
        to whatever's left
of whatever might be remembered—
yet down a ways I hear the creek
still stone-attentive
        and stair-stepping narratives
through the whisk of reeds,
entirely clear-headed and tireless.

The soul lives forever
        but wants to be physical,
wants to touch hickory bark, the spider's silk home,
the warbler on its vibrating throat.

For only a second, the red clay mud...
For only a second, the flint and the shale...

Like anyone else I'm my old addresses too,
the yard-edge apple orchard,
long driveway through the cedar grove,
these and others,
                    back yards and brush piles,
town of little trace on the Tennessee river.

As for life, I've spent the better part
looking for the best part,
                    two streets back
or some such as that, always a little off line.
I'm likely empty, thinking I am filled.

Or else I'm filled
                    with no thoughts cleansed enough
to hold the whatever's been handed them to bear.

September's lament month,
stifle-the-breath month,
                    month looking
for a plausible transition, but none comes.

But I don't care, you hear.
I plan to sit near these elms till I'm drenched
past my honor.
                    Until the light lets loose
of the far clouds. Until I'm moonwashed
and soft-edged,
                    not even the width of a thought.

€ EARLY FALL SANCTUARY

I can't remember autumn starting up.
In which leaf?
                    which sluice of air?

Four in the afternoon, the school bus
makes its stop,
                    children stepping back
into the other life, the one that's been on hold,
that's mostly spent outdoors.

Which child will love the moon
in forty years,
                    which touch his pulse from habit,
which rake his hand across the washing on the line?

We tell ourselves it's not the destination
but the journey,
                    the being-where-one-is.
That's a stretch. That's a get-down-on-one's-knees-
and-feel-around.
                    That's the poetry in us talking.

Meanwhile, something's happened to the sky,
more solitary,
                    more suffused and somber-tinted.
It passes on the closed-up school bus windows,
hushed with being
                    twinned above each bouncing seat.

AN OLD QUARREL PUT TO REST

Bane of the neighborhood, ne'er-do-well,
I can, most evenings, be found near sleep
nursing a half empty glass of ice,
a breeze like breath coming across the porch.
Hostas wither near the dogwood roots.
The deck boards buckle from years of sun.
Long ago, I gave the yard to weeds.
Let them say of me what they will and do,.
for I'm a man of small effect, a monastery
housing many long-robed walking solitudes,
each of them near (or less near) a threshold.
Why fret the flecked paint on porch rails
when one could overhear the thoughts
each bowed head keeps to itself, vessel
of reverence and amplitude, humbly passing through?

The tiniest of mushrooms has sprouted just off the porch.
Three days of rain can banish even the mind.
What happens next feels like a companion
come across Time's plain with news from the Far.
We are safe, at least for now, but a verdict's soon to come.
If wise men came to our door, would we be disregarded?
How long is proper before washing the widow's handkerchief?
It's not possible to live in a world where tree bark doesn't
        instruct.
It's not possible to live in a world without occasional blooms
from the dogwood struck wet and white on the morning
        windshield.
O Life ought to be thrilled with itself, nothing but long hours
and a million bird songs to breathe on its behalf.
Even a bottle cast out along the roadside will see itself
eventually filled. And so will a man if he sits long enough.

LOVE POEM FOR MY BEING HERE AT ALL

When I'm gone, evening still will fall,
the crickets come again
to find this falling porch of stains.
The washstand, propped against a post,
will catch and then release the wind.

Not possible, I know, but still
I've wished to be here
when my absence is the light
walking in and out of sage grass,
nothing there to stall its inarticulation.

But I know better. I know this afternoon
is almost done, and soon I'll rise and go inside
to talk and news and wrung-out dishrags,
the unswept floor I'll sweep and mop
as if this time, for once, the shine can stay.

🕭 LADY OF WEALTH, CIRCA 1963

Obviously when the painter arrived,
she'd already given thought
to how she wished to be revealed.
She wanted, at her side, one bowl,
porcelain of course, and to fit its form
the thin, slumped stem of buttercup.

Brushes and oils he summoned to his hand.
Need we mention her noticing
the delicate quality of his fingers,
or the swell of light on the opposite wall?
She was fugitive from something,
and he would bring her back.

The first marks he made to test the shape
he thought her face would be.
She watched a moving van next door,
an antique dresser mirror, an heirloom surely,
almost tumble from the workers' care.
For a moment it held the long,
curved leaving of street, and then
what seemed—impossible!—
a yellow field beneath a moon.

She found, in the fettered sound
of brush on canvas, a jubilation.
And how she envied him, this artist,
seeking what's divine, who spent his hours
companion to the faint, accruing layers.

What would she tell her friends
when they returned from trips abroad

to find her likeness window-large
and placed upon the mantel?

Flick of wrist. Dab and swirl.
Submerge and surface. Once begun,
when's a new creation to find its finish?
When turned for inspection? When dry?

He has leaned in close and whispered
in her ear—someone has—
or else it could be almost any prompt
that's set her there on white
with downcast eyes, like one assembled,
like one who's been away and now,
recalling a former script,
remembers why she ventured out.

MID-FALL SANCTUARY

One day, when no one knows to listen,
my voice
      will fade out toward the silence
it always loved,
always felt surrounded by.

The next week's rains will come,
will rivulet toward the roots
              withering a little less.
What's hidden or known will alter only slightly,
if at all. What's unknown will still be tantamount.

Today, though, I drag my feet
toward the everlasting
           and the shucked-off light
I have to look at twice
not to think I am suddenly elsewhere.

I love how an hour can be or dissolve.
I love how the mind
           wants to know what it knows.
Even when we cease, the tint on the leaves increases,
the wind slow-turns its calculations on the grassy field,
sometimes cicada-shrill, sometimes blank sky,
sometimes moment
           flushed of all narrative.

MORNING AND NIGHT

Beyond our town the bottomlands flood each year.
Someone's son goes walking, never comes back.
Weeks pass. Town square talk reclaims the days.

Tonight I hear the rain remember roots
and think of elders gone the long way back to dust.
What we know by heart we doubt the most.

I have a wish to be at someone's door,
unannounced but welcomed anyway, ushered in
to dine and sing and sleep the sleep of kings.

But this is a world of slaughtered saints.
Random shots are fired, while morning and night
our mothers turn their faces toward the sleeping hills.

So quickly has the century come and gone.
For a while let's ask each other simple questions
and make up answers that can keep us home tonight.

REPLY TO THE SHHH IN THE NOVEMBER GRASS

This conversation started years and years ago,
before the wind dipped low
                                            to hedge and brushstroke
overlooked leaves, before the light set out
on its way to restitution.

It'll get there and then some,
the able light, the without-fade light.
I'd take it in my veins
                                if I could grasp
a thin start, a little burn toward the bone.

Already cool this morning, but the rain
cooled us more. Not quite to the core, though.
Not quite to the core.
                                Upwind and downwind,
I let myself wander in absentia,
moved toward tree-shine
                                and rinsings of leaves.

The family elders line up for their deaths,
down the dirt roads,
                                out along the ridges.
Newspapers tuck their names near the folds,
and town square talk
                                nips at all our etymologies.

I think this narrow path
                                keeps narrowing as I go:
root-clump and moss-bank, hollow and hollow.
Soon there won't be space to find a step.

And what can be done,

                    what can be said,

when the empty garden won't hold a rose,

when the boundless can't accept a pin-prick,

when the blank page

                    has no room for a word?

AMONG THE GIANTS OF EAST MAIN POOL HALL

"Rack 'em," some grease-haired shark would strut and say,
nodding the tip of his stick at my face to taunt
and tease me up, the next in line to lose.
I admit that in his eyes I was a runt,
of little consequence—he'd mostly sigh
or laugh when I'd miscue or try to pose
like Minnesota Fats. My shots went wide.
Runs? One ball long. I was sitting-duck dead.

But oh I loved the smell of chalk on cues
and the green felt I ran my hand across.
I couldn't bank a shot to save my life,
or gain respect. My stance had no pizzazz.
While smack-talk filled the air, I'd fantasize
the eight ball sunk, no way to get out safe.

SEQUEL TO WHITMAN'S "I SAW IN LOUISIANA A LIVE OAK GROWING"

I saw a live oak, too,
twisted from the base,
            a supple, sliding curve of trunk
that brought the eye toward heaven.

The eye can never tire of going there, I say
and having said it
            wonder if I'm wrong,
since so often what I know
is less than half of what could be.

I cannot help but say
            its limbs were undulations,
though somehow constant and without the least of mimicry,
also overlapping and entwined.

I thought the earth must have a love of line
the way a painter does,
            touching forth a shape
to trace the traces of whatever's in between—
all form a conversation with the fact or lack of God.

I'm of the bark and roots, of the bulk of limbs,
of the kneeling down I do
            to see how best to stand.
I'm grafted to the farthest reaching leaf,
there where the sky-shine's soon eclipsed,
where the next bud's foray
            tests the white and blue.

LATELY ENOUGH TO MATTER

Startled awake by wind chimes,
the grandmother rises
and steps onto the side porch.
She still has her senses,
the bitter and sweet on her tongue,
the wind-found fine hairs at the nape.
Now, not even tired, she waits
for coming light, hours of sky.
She deeply breathes the wind-swell.
After thirty years the trees are like
old friends whose familiar movements
she's decided she will miss in the next life.

EARLY WINTER SANCTUARY

Finally, the first frost. On the ground.
In the trees. Breath becomes a shape outside us
lingering for a moment
                          in its visible form.

Let's speak of song and where it takes us,
speak insurrections
                          in the heart of the heart,
wholeness not as some ideal but touchable,
like a sleeve, a coffee pot, an eyelash.

Take down the book that reeks of love
and says its words
                          cannot be ascertained by human tongue.
Say them anyway. Say the least and the most,
then put the book aside
                          and be its aftertrace.

The maple's always last accepting vacancy.
Its underlimbs—gnarled but gorgeous, thickened—
stand braced against
                          the season's certain snows.
The mind hears *hush, hush.* And it does.

TO LORCA

I'm told you passed a summer residence
for children when they took you to your death.
It comes, I know, as little recompense,
but I've prayed for you and wondered, when breath
no longer held, if those who stood above
their still-warm guns could smell the olive grove.
I'd like to think they turned—*a whisper?*—dared
the shadows, the sky, looked to where you stared.
But you and I—far-fetched—already were
in conversation across the years. No way
to silence that. In my room, on display,
your words still meet a harsher world with gestures
it reviles. I'd call them mine, if that could
cause the guards to take their eyes from where you stood.

THE POET WHO NEVER ACHIEVED

No matter—dreaming still, he walked his room,
a steady pace, and seized upon some words
that knew their windblown strength,
                              like certain birds
that writhe in downdrafts but soar beyond their doom.

He read his betters, praised them when he could
and sought to make them better known, though few
could know this fact, not knowing him,
                              who knew
it best this way. The years stretched on, withstood

the poems he offered up; and when he died,
the movers boxed his things and never knew
that thirty years of poems fell into flame
and were consumed.
                    No matter—words abide.

Even the ones put down so brief renew
the world somehow—toward loss, toward lack of fame.

Hey, folks, don't blame me.
We'd all be rich
        and full of spunk
if I had my say.
We'd let the sky in, for once,
            on *our* secrets,
instead of staring up at stars and black hole hints,
through quarks and space dust,
          wishing we knew what's what.

If I had my say,
        we'd spend all day on hillsides,
slantwise-walking, advancing a careless narrative.
But none exists. Not really. Not careless, at least.

And the stars are more than incidentals.
We hear a word spoken
        and smooth out our souls.
Each night keeps its day tucked back in a fold
and pulls it out
        just when it seems there's no chance
for light. But don't blame me.

I've done what I could with the little I've had.
I've sat up long past the dark night
and still couldn't catch
        the light-stunned moment
when suddenly yards and streets were *seen*
—bucket by the flower bed, shovel against the oak—
all of it light-bathed,
        light-splintered and -gentled,
the light on its way already here and going.

✍ ELDER POET'S FINAL TOUR

He has only *this* poem, this one chance
to pull us in and maybe have us
love him or at least acknowledge
we'll go down together when we're
finished here—this flawed and quaint attempt—
here where, at least for now, no one's being
dragged and flogged upon our city's streets,
no one bears the grief of mothers
lost to drink, no one's labeled undesirable,
where the weather's balmy, and we're soon to hug
the strangers left and right. Just *this* poem
—he's been working his whole life
to find the words to keep us near,
to turn our faces back to something
whispered and believed between us.
We have more pressing obligations,
the trance-like prattles of our minds
which have carried us to where we are
and are as valid as the light
we touch, the air we breathe.
He has these words he's fiddled with,
and the evening soon will close its doors,
and we will walk out to our separate lives
along some sullen street where if we meet,
we might exchange a passing word,
no more, then hurry forth
to where it is we think we have to be.

BREATHING EXERCISE

That poet named Anonymous—maybe he, or she, had it right:
what claim can anyone have when right words come along?
After all, it's not one's name that alters the girl's sense
of herself, when she's stolen in among the burdened stacks.

And while we're at it, let us imagine the long night
through which the insomniac counts his many selves.
Perhaps if many breathe in measure on his behalf,
he'll close his eyes and be again in that meadow he desires.

What we give the world deserves suspicion, an old man
bitter and poor, mumbling about the size of his woodpile.
We expect ovation, long applause, generous predictions,
yet the ash pan is full, needs dumping past the barn.

Someone has to point us toward the intimate. Someone needs
to know a harp's faint sound in the background when soldiers
start door to door. Oh why don't we admit we're exhausted?
It takes great effort not to shout for joy when we see each other.

POEM OF THE EARTH

I was told to guard my step
against the snakes that roamed
the undergrowth and stretched
to sun themselves along
the road back up the hill.
No one had to tell me:
the fear was in my bones,
divinely put there by
a God who knows young boys
will traipse off anywhere.
Every field was mine,
no matter who had bought
the right to call it theirs.
I recognized the wind
and rain and sunlight slants
that came down through the trees
as if to point my way—
go here and here and here.
No one had to set me down
and tell me I belonged
or make some storied lesson
of the earth's abundant love
for me and all who walk
upon it. I knew already,
for the earth had told me so;
and I knew, too, that even
twenty miles from town
on land that very few
could find, when I stood
beside the creek, I stood
beside the sea of Galilee.
Great storms amassed and then

were calmed. Men walked and sank
and walked again and prayed
ferociously, so that I heard
their words upon the wind.
I took them as my own
and hid them in my heart,
believing that the fall of man,
though harsh and often lonely,
gave us sky to contemplate
and streams in which to dip
our burning hands and tongues.
Say what you will about
this life, the little time
we get to call it ours—
it's always something new
and sweet, not a morning
or an afternoon that isn't
weighted down with more than we
could ever hope to carry back,
hopeless as we are yet home.
Warned to keep a look-out,
I did, and have, and what
I've seen convinces me
I shall not ever want,
though men demand of me
everything I have or am,
careless men, men who thrust
their faces at the days and balk,
cursing and despising them.
Say what you will about
the passing of this day
or any other day
that blesses you with time,
the sun, a trail to walk—

the steps we take are pressed
forever to the earth,
and sometimes rain collects
and small birds come to drink.

AUTHOR'S NOTE

Jeff Hardin was born in Savannah, Tennessee, and educated at Austin Peay State University and the University of Alabama. He is the author of two chapbooks, *Deep in the Shallows* (GreenTower Press) and *The Slow Hill Out* (Pudding House). Nominated numerous times for the Pushcart Prize, his poems appear in *The New Republic, Ploughshares, Mid-American Review, Ascent, Zone 3, West Branch* and others. He teaches at Columbia State Community College in Columbia, Tennessee.